Life, Sex & Death

A Poetry Collection (Vol 1)

By David Ellis

Intro/Preface

Thank you for purchasing this book and welcome to my first poetry collection.

In here you will find a veritable smorgasbord of adventure, excitement, romance, philosophy and lashings of comedy served up in a wicked concoction of rhyme and verse.

My poetry takes cues from many random different things like popular art, film, food, music and culture, social media, political commentary, family, relationships and emotional abstract concepts. I'm sure that there is something here for everyone.

I have grouped them all together based on their dominant themes of Love/Romance, Philosophical (where most of my more comedic musings take place) and Inspirational for your own ease of reference.

I sincerely hope you find a wealth of inspiration, humour and kindred spirits in these poetic pieces. They were all written with a singular purpose in mind, as regardless of the subject matter, they should move you emotionally and in the vast majority of cases put a song in your heart and a smile on your face or act as cathartic remedy to sensitive issues in your life.

I have also published a debut Short Story Collection called "A Little Bit of What You Fancy", so if you enjoy my writing then please take a look at it. It's available on Amazon Kindle and in print.

If you are interested in further updates regarding my work, feel free to become a follower on Twitter or subscribe to my blog. My Twitter handle is **@TooFullToWrite** and my blog can be found at www.toofulltowrite.com.

Cover design by David Ellis (Cover Photo by Friza Reihan at www.fancycrave.com)

Copyright © 2016 by David Ellis. 2nd Edition.

Publisher – CreateSpace Publishing.

For permission requests, write to the author at the e-mail address provided in the 'About the Author' page.

Please support the author by reviewing this book on Amazon, Goodreads and Barnes & Noble.

About the Author

David Ellis is an author of poetry, fiction and music lyrics.

He lives in Tunbridge Wells, Kent in the UK.

David is extremely fond of cats and dogs but not snakes.

Indiana Jones is his spirit animal.

He can be contacted at davidellisauthor@gmail.com

Contents

Inspirational

Abstract Acrostalyptica
August 2013

Arranging life to fit the whims of others, a chimerical, misguided nirvanA

Businesslike in one's actions, verbosely brusque, a sensual ancient proverB

Chaos ensues, tragic, a waterfall on the senses, potent aphrodisiaC

Disciplined enigmas, on a fatal collision course, heralded, foretolD

Exact hits the spot, absolute, to the point of being just adequatE

Framed for crimes of being yourself, guilty of a Mexican StandofF

Guided by a groovy hedonistic beat, so alluring is the rhythmic cravinG

Harmonious in gesture but sequestered in saucy chutzpaH

Immaculate, delicate nature but still naively greener than any broccolI

Juggling with all of these thoughts that spin, rub, scratch, maniacal DJ

King of all you survey, there are worlds you must conquer, quicK

Logical though it may seem, lucidity a fleeting dream, exhilarating cocktaiL

Meticulously flowing, a stream for all seasons, fiercely gaining momentuM

Neatly numbered numbness, too rigid means denying any chaos is inhumaN

Overseeing judgement calls, future conundrums rage, a runaway tornadO

Painstakingly firm, love's beacon shines through, bittersweet backdroP

Qualities employed without fear of searing the conscience like a BBQ

Rational, romantic ideals struggle for the right audience, they overpoweR

Sandwiched plainly between an illustrious crust, fervent lust procrastinateS

Tethered, tranquil insidiousness runs deep into vulnerable veins, reticenT

Unmistakeable intensity, threatening to engulf, consume before its plateaU

Veracious creatures we are, manipulating feelings, a play worthy of ChekoV

Working in subtle ways, defining ourselves, pieces missing, perfect jigsaW

X-Rays of our lives highlight crystal clear hues, an ornamental paradoX

Years yielding an essence flavoured by positive actions have no boundarY

Zodiacal, we're animals, embracing the nature of our characters with pizazZ

Attitude Without Spite
April 2014

My code is simple

It is very easy to follow

If you listen closely then I'm sure you will find

No-one can bring you down

Attitude without spite

Will see you right

Respect and trust

The women in your life

Be honest in all of your dealings

Empathise with others' feelings

Discover exciting new abilities

Reconnect with old ones frequently

Flow around problems

Take them in your stride

Adapt to situations

Remain sensitive, kind and wise

Embody generosity with gifts

Share knowledge freely

Plant good seeds in others

Let them grow and multiply

Never be afraid to challenge

The regimental status quo

Following all rules to the letter

Makes things no fun at all

If you are having problems

Try to tackle them head on

Benevolence is ultimately the key

To dealing with the ignorant few

So hold your head up high

Stay proud of who you are

Look life dead in the eye and say

"I'm ready for this adventure!"

Never quit, never give up, work hard

Achieve everything you could ever want

No-one is ever going to stop you

Trust me, it is going to be impossible

All you have to do is be a force of good

Then spend the rest of your life enjoying the rewards

Bare Your Heart
June 2014

Fill your days with joy

At every opportunity

Before it is too late

Dispense with envy

For it is your enemy

Stop living a life of hate

Pity the fools

That cannot embrace

The love that others give

When consumed by rage

Let it all fall away

Until nothing but peace remains

Do not fear of the unknown

Ignore it and press on

It should never hold you back

When dwelling in sadness

Take a moment to reminisce

Yet never let it control your fate

If you find yourself courting disgust

Be careful that you are not

Subjecting people to your own prejudice

Cherish compassion and truth

Then more people will respect you

To the point where you feel blessed

Surprise others often

Give them a sense of appreciation

Be the gift of light that shines deep into their lives

Friendship and courage

Employed throughout the ages

Passed on from Father and Mother

To sons and daughters

Virtues that stand the test of time

Be In Their Lives Today
January 2013

You roll the dice of life, sire a son or a daughter

Steer, navigate, through a sea of troubled waters

Invoking courage, discipline, avoiding serious scolding

Encouraging latent talents to keep unfolding, evolving

The awards they receive make you so pleased

Maybe one day they will dare to grow up to be

Everything you had hoped for, wished for or ever dreamed

Not a nightmarish caricature of evil or a cartoonish beast

Splurging out on clothes and expensive I-Phones

Chasing latest fads because their friends said so

Your musical tastes are old-fashioned, you're not cool

Why aren't you more 'down with it' like kids at school?

First love blossoms, their teenage crush beckons

On standby to pick up the pieces at any second

University, job, marriage, a car, the housing ladder

Parent now grandparent, a new experiment in terror

But a funny thing happens, a transformation occurs

Time replaced with memories, hopes, dreams, purpose

All of the fears and frustrations fall away from the core

Living vicariously through younger lives, you feel reborn

You wouldn't change it for anything in the world

When it's good, you soar higher than the clouds

The smiles, laughter, the cherished looks on their face

Erases all the bad vibes of life's unavoidable mistakes

A child will never ever be a means to an end

The journey matters more than the destination

Love unconditional, thick, thin, sorrow and regret

An experience those without can't comprehend yet

Sometimes the breeding bit is the hardest part

The rest is just science

Be Your Own Inspiration
March 2015

Sick of being my own worst critic

Rushing around like a frantic lunatic

Life unwinds at such a tumultuous pace

Make your mark or leave without a trace

So many times I've told myself

Don't live the life of someone else

Just stay true to what matters most to you

Go wild, cut loose and experience renewal

Hearts and minds can feel confused and abused

When terrible events crop up in the news

It gets so much that we should all turn it off

Escape to create a world without conflict or hate

Be the rainbow that adorns the skies

When love's involved, don't think twice

Seize the mood and take your time

Fun shouldn't come with a deadline

If you know what you want, just go for it

You're taking a chance, not making a mistake

There's a rhyme and a reason for everything

Settle for nothing less than perfection

Be your own inspiration

Conundrums
April 2014

Why do we tend to love the things that don't love us back?

Why do we always want the things that we cannot have?

Why does the sun shine when we want it to rain?

Why is it that heartache is the worst kind of pain?

How can you truly tell if someone really likes you?

How can suffering be worthwhile if it's for a selfish goal?

How do you profoundly make a difference in someone's world?

How do you do it in a way to make your own family proud?

What can we do when the universe decides to cause havoc and hell?

What can we learn from those who choose to betray our goodwill?

What can we see in others that we would like to mirror in ourselves?

What must be done to make our inner light shine above all else?

Why does time run like sand through desperate fingers?

Why do best laid plans sometimes crumble all around us?

Why can't we distinguish between opinion and good advice?

Why don't we cherish the friends who help us through life?

How can we understand feelings more ancient than buildings?

How do we build foundations of peace and understanding?

How many more times must we go back to the beginning?

How can we acknowledge that change has to come from within?

When will it become apparent that we are not all competing?

When will things slow down enough so our heads aren't constantly spinning?

When do we know when to stop judging ourselves to impossible standards?

When do we jump off this train so we can find out some certain answers?

Why do breath-taking dreams often fade just after we wake?

Why are memories the most vibrant when remembering mistakes?

Why decide to stick to one course of action when many exist?

Why limit yourself when you have the power of choice?

A Cosmic Pillar
October 2014

The light within all of us can triumph over darkness

Celebrate the natural birth of exciting new beginnings

No hating of negatives, if they bring positive changes

We can succeed where others have failed before us

New knowledge doesn't have to replace ancient scripts

It binds and enhances old techniques and experiences

If you can bounce back from every setback harder than before

Whether it be major or minor, you're building character

Exchanging gifts between family members and close friends

A time of remembering how to love your fellow man and woman

The sun shines on, a cosmic pillar, a beacon of buttery purity

Bringing energy to life, plants, animals and people majestically

Legends, myths and stories surface about good versus evil

The enduring tales feature those who ultimately become heroes

Fighting ignorance wherever they see it, with much compassion

Fearlessly removing obstacles of injustice that are plain wrong

Music, literature and learning free you from self-imposed prisons

Never doubt your own unique abilities or question the nature of them

Relationships and friendships are what matter the most

Devote some time to bringing happiness to the hearts of others

And you will truly find happiness in yourself above all else

The Creative Horizon Where No-One Else Has Been
June 2015

The direction of the wind

Always lets us know who we really are

Helps us to see all of the truly beautiful things

In a world that cannot easily be touched

Love and cherish the moments that you share

When the energy spreads

The boundaries that were once lost in forbidden dreams

Are now constantly shifting, evolving

Reinventing and redefining within the blink of an eye

The measures of who we are

Allow for the occasional mistake

Freedom comes from the many choices

That others often fail to find the courage to make

We can judge people on

The harvest that they bring in

Yet, if you pay your own way

By bringing happiness, compassion and kindness into lives

Then it's obvious who is the richer man or woman

If by preparing for the worst

Means that we do our absolute best today

Our tears won't be in vain or born of pain

They will be tears of joy

Inspiring others as they bathe in this glorious rain

Out of problems grow humble solutions

Opportunities may not present themselves at convenient times

However, nothing ever determines where you can go

It merely determines where you can start from

This is where you can make all the difference

Where the sun sets as it prepares to rise again

Thought is your wind, so sail onward valiantly to success my friends

Let your heart take charge, as you conquer the journey within

Do Whatever Works For You
February 2014

Back to the drawing board

I've made it this far

I'm never giving up

I draw my sword

Bare my soul to paper

The first cut is always the deepest

Phrases sear delicately across my brain

A dialogue exchange of fire and brimstone

No mercy for the weak

Only the strong survive and thrive

Dipping my beak in salty waters

Drowning for almost an eternity

Ghostly siren whispers from across the sea

Softly seducing me until I can't breathe

Fighting against the cold darkness of the mirror's edge

Reflections of boundaries, forbidden worlds

Blood spent, spilled, all over the battlefield

A war without sound, only echoes of dreams

So sweet, plucked from the divine vineyards

To connect the dots has now become impossible

Your sensual touch remains forever unattainable

All I see is mystery behind guarded eyes

Temptation's vintage thirst quenched

Answers turned up that were meaningless, dead ends

Yet, while things will never be the same

Change brings its own reward

And the price of immortality

A Double Edged Sword
February 2013

Pride can be a sword

That can stab you in the back

Don't be the one

To take the fall

If confidence is what you lack

Hate can be a mistake

A jealous enemy you can forsake

Consumed by evil

You derail your goals

Hampering any progress you make

Be proud of yourself

Focus on all your achievements

Look at how far

That you have come

The lives touched now have purpose

Face your fears

Your mind is now crystal clear

An ocean of serene calm

Where once was a storm

Now you're the pilot and the bombardier

Asking for help

Is not a weakness

And neither is

Helping others

So wear your proudness

On your sleeves

And remember

To inspire others

As they have done for you

A perfect circle

That makes us all complete

No need to compete

No need for anger, fear, loathing

Just love and peace

Dreams Are Worth Saving
February 2013

Things are passed up, ignored, when they should be
desired

Abandoned, ditched by the road, cars with slashed tyres

They sit frozen, fossilised, numb, awaiting absolution

Scars forged deep, seared, blunt and fuelled with emotion

Sacrificing dreams for safe hands of financial stability

Wishing that chance would just show us all a little mercy

A fickle operator, a dice roll we all have gambled on

The triumph of human spirit, we just start all over again

Leaves from trees of knowledge fall through inquisitive
fingers

Droplets of hope, nourishment, encouragement, held
prisoner, linger

Aching and yearning for their ultimate release

To dine on sumptuous purpose and to be set free

But if we smother/choke aspirations to an undeserved death

Left to perish in the quagmire of a slavishly tepid life

All the bucket lists in the world will do you no good

If passion is bereft and your ambition has been killed

We tell our loved ones that it was a good effort in trying

Are we the ones though, to whom ultimately we are lying?

Convincing ourselves that we are earning earthly redemption

When courage has faltered and we're yielding to temptation

Sinking further and deeper into a quicksand maze

With no-one to guide us out from this foolish haze

Consumed by excess, we are forced to acquiesce, to give up

Squeezed by greed but without dreams, it will never be enough

If any dreams are truly worth saving

It's through the lives of our children

They have the energy, power, the passion

Worst case scenario, we will die trying

But through them our legacy still lives on

Embrace Your Impetuousness
March 2014

Acting on a shared consciousness

Neither of us can resist

Why play it safe in life

When everything is at stake

Moments should be seized

At every available opportunity

To establish who we are

Before we start fading fast

Love can be all consuming

Journeying deep from within

Indifferent yet compassionate

Fragile but with a heart of diamond

Embracing the beauty of all things

Sending every emotion to heaven

Animal instincts begin kicking in

Overflowing our senses to the brim

We all have our own drives

Lusts, desires and our reasons

Trying to hide what's inside

Simply because we fear rejection

Yet to take one small step

Takes courage of our convictions

Drawing confidence from surroundings

Hope nurtured until it gives birth

Mother nature gave us the tools

To allow us to conquer all

The only challenge that we face day to day

Is to ignore our own suffering and humility

We can be everything

We've ever set out to be

As long as we act on our impulses

Before it's too late

There are no mistakes

Just choices we didn't make

Doing nothing isn't a crime

But when romance is on the cards

Don't hesitate to ask

And whether we sink or swim

At least we will die happy

At the world's end of our time

Eucalyptus Consciousness
March 2015

Never despair, for knowledge itself

Puts power in the hands of the warrantor

Those who celebrate sincerity

Will burn more brightly than any stars

Hope brings out the champion

To conquer any sticky situation

Be the chance as thin as a hair

Or thick as a pint of blood

Find a directional path in life

Channel focus, favour durableness

Overdressing your intentions

Means gravitating towards disaster

Appearances can be deceptive, protested

Yet I find there is always truth in wine

A babbler can distort perceptions

Just like a creamer can discolour coffee beans

What nourishes can also destroy if used gluttingly

To fear success is to be squirmingly surrogated

In a life that thrives on passionate engagement

Not knowing if we're removably attached or removably secured

Messes with our minds, we become shallow, unable to commit

Yet we are all bound by our actions and our art

Imitate but do not loathe the worlds you create

An interword cannot convey meaning with half measures

He or she who gives twice as much deserves just rewards

Going Beyond Limitations
November 2013

Natural evolution favours adopters of classical wisdom

Exotic spheres of catastrophes collide, random associations

To know thyself is to embrace compassion

Keep everything within a degree of moderation

Opportunities should rule the heart, not mind

Impossible or not, attempts must be tried

Patience brings respect, honour, a noble life

Nothing is accidental if you just believe

Ancient wonders uncovered never cease to amaze

Music so sweet, electrifying, painting the air

We're all more than names or numbers

To express yourself is the ultimate goal

Failures forgotten, hard work brings success now

Never allow negativity to gain ultimate control

Essence of our struggles is knowing, understanding

Making connections, building friendships, bridges, deeper meanings

Dreamers and intellectual explorers of the obscure

An abstract world with no clear answers

Life is to be felt and experienced

Triumphing over adversity however harrowing the circumstance

Allowing divine silence to surrender its secrets

Create a core around which everything revolves

Time for everything, just let it unfold

Pick what's important, outsmart the status quo

Balance between holding on and letting go

No such thing as an overactive imagination

Just people pushing for elimination of innovation

Achieve so much more going beyond limitations

Integrity's Touch
February 2014

Atrociously immaculate

The lasting effect that

You have on the world

Can be broken in an instant

If integrity's touch is severed

Exquisitely destitute

Digging for deeper meanings

Human nature at its most complex

Unfathomable in its context

In seas of convoluted dreams

Deliciously quaint, ancient

Different ways of coping

A maelstrom of emotions

With only one-way out

Onwards into battle

Perilously silent

Unyielding to anything

Slaying diabolical inhibitions

Preventing you from achieving

Lofty goals and ambitions

Tradition dictates

That to leave an enduring legacy

One must have lead

A life deemed to be worthy

So above all else

Be yourself

Don't let anyone

Poison the well

Be prolific, kind and generous

And if that doesn't work

Tell the universe to back off

At least until we've finished this glass

Cheers!

Into The Stars
April 2015

As fish years ago, we drank the flood waters to save the world

We seek signs of salvation in everything, even boxes of cereal

Legends take pleasure in telling us the answers we think we need

But ask the right questions and you can avoid stampeding crowds

There are no stars burning brighter than intellect you display

You can be beautiful too but there is no need to be vain

A complex plot develops but the outcome is still the same

Die at the hands of pregnant precaution

Or embrace risk and live to fight another day

Advice should be heeded to prevent a heart of stone

A phoenix can only rise from the ashes of noble bones

Imitations may fool you with their vicious sleights of hand

Don't let yourself be a target or bury your head into the sand

A tree bearing fruit cannot be pierced by a sword or spear

An empty shell filled with passion will still make sounds divine to hear

Domesticated at birth does not mean sterile as an adult

Separate the animal from the rider, in order to channel sparks

There is much to learn below the horizon in the seas and in the skies

Descended from the very Gods and Goddesses themselves

We can be the ones to shine, we just have to believe in ourselves

Life And Growth
April 2014

Going toe to toe

Against life's roulette wheel

Spinning scenarios

Until my number comes up

It's not about winning any more

Or deciding who keeps score

Each side has players

Rules are now outdated

What's wrong with this picture

When the pieces don't fit together

There used to be a single idea

Before it got complicated with fear

We speak without meaning

So our sacrifices mean nothing

Asking for mercy

Being rewarded with stress

To succeed in restoring

Former past glories

Perception must be altered

New paths must be forged

The sun will rise again

Thorns can be removed from paws

Rhythms can return to normal

Growth through strength and wisdom

Courage to face new challenges

Change may be difficult to accept

You make your own luck in this life

With honour, dignity and respect

It's up to you to hit the jackpot

Love Who You Are
September 2014

I wonder, I ponder

At the splendour of this world

How it can be so beautiful and so fragile

Achingly gorgeous yet coldly brutal

A gilded lily encased with fire in its belly

Ready to explode at a moment's notice

Unless it's handled with care and respect

I puzzle over, I dare to reflect

That to love someone

Can be such an enormous gamble

The stakes so breathtakingly high and if it dies

Its death sinks you to profound, rock-bottom lows

Yet it's always worth the risks involved

Just to taste its sweet essence when it works

Its purity enough for a thousand lifetimes

I contemplate, I deliberate

How time can be so precious

Yet so very easy to waste

On things that don't deserve it

Procrastination, infatuation, legislation

Heartache, sorrow and unnecessary pain

To let go can be difficult

Yet to stay the same borders on insane

I dwell, I mull over

The tragedies that befall us

Bereavement, disease, war

Famine, murder and divorce

How much stronger we can become

When the occasion is called for

That the human spirit can be crushed

Beaten and even left for dead

Yet like a phoenix it rises from the ashes

I speculate and envisage a desire

For an easier, happier, care-free life

One filled with less stress and less strife

Yet it is our own trials and tribulations

That ultimately define us

Colouring us in, for better or for worse

We carry these scars because we must

This is who we are

This is who we are destined to be

Wearing our hearts and minds on our sleeves

This is the cost of passion, of raw emotions

Love who you are and never look back

Modern Ragnarök
April 2014

Sparks set the world ablaze

Icy claws freeze the sun

Blinding us with a golden haze

Dreams of death bring wisdom

Only the strongest tales survive

Built from foundations of flesh and bone

Azure oceans froth and writhe

Crashing wildly into the unknown

Bestowing a name to our pain

Ancient myths and prophesies

Retreating off this terrain

Fighting against past mistakes

Pursuing knowledge from the Gods

Moving mountains with ease

Time and elements collide

The land is fertile and green

As our scars run deep

We must embrace our fate

Don't be a source of war

Let go of all your hate

We may be friends, lovers or foes

You play your part in a bigger design

As we kiss the glowing stars

The light that fills us tastes divine

Calm the angry fires in your heart

Dare to soar on the crest of emotions

Love like there is no end in sight

Explode with compassion, affection and devotion

Take roots and stand firm

Born a wolf, die a righteous person

Passage of A Rolling Stone
April 2014

Never happier

Than when I'm moving my feet

My passport to adventure

Keeps desire burning inside of me

I could be learning

Ancient cultures or forgotten histories

Soaking up vivid stories

People's lives enshrouded in mystery

Making new memories

Just as the old ones begin to fade

On display in my mind as trophies

These journeys are now crusades

I never thought that

When I was growing up

I would place so much importance

On exploring new worlds

When you expand your mind

Take in fresh continents and sights

Horizons become broadened

Experiences take on a bolder light

I found that

Love comes in many guises

An appreciation of art

Transcends all languages

The messages we give out

Can often get confusing

We take unnecessary shortcuts

Trying to reclaim wasted time

When our focus should be in the moment

Exploring further ways to vary mundane rituals

Take flight on a whim, try somewhere different

Pleasure you can't measure, infinitely medicinal

The Price Of Greatness Is The Price Of Responsibility
May 2015

There's a war simmering behind the scenes

We are fighting it on the beaches every day

It clouds our hearts, minds, hopes and our dreams

Living vicariously on a crash collision course

Through misguided fear, loathing and jealousy

What causes people to pick up guns, knives and weapons

And claim it is all in the name of peace is beyond me

Stirring up a gamut of emotions both physically and mentally

A hypocritical stance to be taken in the extreme

There is no room for this type of behaviour

In a civilised society leaving behind the dark ages

If you have got a gripe concerning your beliefs

Use your hands and brain to write something

Work with the people that try to protect you

Laws are there for a reason, to not let us resort to raping and killing

Don't justify your own personal suffering with violent expression

You will not be seen as a martyr but as a monster for certain

Courage is what counts and how we adapt to change

It's what amounts to real currency in any debate

Often we need to learn how to sit down and listen

If we are to make any kind of difference

Honour, duty, justice, freedom, mercy and hope

These are the qualities that we need to show

There should be no desire to thrive on conflict

For without the constant pressures of humanity

We are merely empty shells, hollow vessels, zombies

To succeed we must do what is necessary

Shaping history and leaving a dignified legacy

The empire of the future needs to leave bloodshed behind

The price of greatness is the price of responsibility

A Public Toast To Your Health
February 2013

There is an argument here, for and against

Public vs private, your health in the balance

You can ignore the government hand out

And pay with money from your own belt

I would gladly sacrifice more tax in my salary

Ensuring the privilege did not stay only with me

As if I'm employed then I consider myself lucky

I'm in a position to cover myself financially

Since if the shoe was on the other foot

How are you going to afford private?

If you lost everything, your job, home, your family

Where's your guarantee that things will be alright?

Shouldn't be trapeze artists with no nets

Daredevils flying against life's wind with no sails

Competition among privates means better services

But it's going to be of ill use if you can't afford it

We all grow old and get weak before we die

Life could be taken from us at a moment's notice

Why make things more complicated

By removing one in favour of fiscal merits

Yes, there are queues on the NHS (or Medicaid in the US)

Because many need help that they sorely cannot get

If you take that away from them and hand them a bill

You give them a whole new, desperate kind of peril

We need a foundation to fall back upon

It's money well spent knowing that

Others less fortunate may benefit

Even if we don't regularly use it

So why not run both, then everyone wins

With you helping out your fellow human beings

To me that has got to be the greatest feeling

To have and not need, until the time is right

A consequence of saving lives

A Road Ravaged By Thoughts
April 2015

All that I believe in and all I am not

Pain follows a road ravaged by thoughts

Bridging the gap between existence and death

Rivers form seas as we take our last breaths

Never have I seen such a terrible, tragic waste

When loved ones are seized from us in their prime

Sometimes we don't even get to say our goodbyes

So they sell us their memories, one at a time

We've got nowhere to run and nowhere to hide

Freedom of choice can often be a choice denied

Nothing is that simple with the world weighing down

Finding yourself is impossible if you don't want to be found

Past and future can collide, become a blur

Neither here nor there, they both just merge

Yet death makes it possible for life to be a gift

As long as we accept consequences of our own actions

Nobody will blame you if you want to give up

Who are we to criticise, who are we to judge?

Things reach a point though where a stand must be made

To go out fighting just like our loved ones did, unafraid

So why don't we continue to make them all proud

By doing no wrong on this path that is well-travelled

Heartache and sorrow may hinder us at first

Yet the triumph of human spirit gives wings to our words

Sending them to the heavens to the ones we adore

Connecting us to their gentle touch for now and forever

This Story Starts Today
August 2014

The fire in my heart does rage

A new page of this story starts today

For all these years, I've been afraid

Now I can look destiny in the eye once again

The past may have been a treacherous road

Full of heartache and creepy shadows

It's finally time to swallow it all

Fear and hate no longer taking their toll

Live and learn the same lesson

Or flow with change in other directions

Nothing to slow you down or to hold you back

Drawing energy from people and surroundings from the fat of the land

Fill yourself up on Euphorian kisses

Embracing the raw power that love brings

For each day brings countless new opportunities

Each negative leads to many positives

Ride and tame a flexible mantra

Flow like the gorgeous green and blue hues of the ocean

Continue to put out good things in determined, perpetual waves

Kindness, generosity and undying love

Watch it all come surging back to you threefold

These are the stories that never get old

This is why storytellers are both made and conceived

This is why you never give up, if you want to fulfil your dreams

When The Tornado Strikes
April 2015

Today is the right day to put everything on the line

Ignore heartache and fear, letting confidence be your guide

All of those risks that you failed to take yesterday morning

Now is the chance to roll the dice, throw caution to the wind

Indecisiveness creates stagnation of your progress

Procrastination only protects you from perceived loss

Heroes are the ones to make sacrifices in their lives

Ensuring wonder, adventure, spontaneous delight

Start a new business or leave home, take the bull by the horns

There are always paths through, no matter how formidable

Break boundaries of society's own anxieties

Have courage in all your own ideas and abilities

Losing is acceptable if you learn from your mistakes

Never give up on your dreams or face being lost at sea

Be willing to drop everything in a heartbeat for love

When the tornado strikes look it straight in the eye each time

Own the space, don't be swayed by negative opinion

The difference between success and failure is small

Lives only improve when we decide to make the first move

Death is not the greatest concern here in this random game

What distinguishes us from all the rest is uniqueness

Embrace the present moment and shape it to stay alive

A World Of Make-Believe
December 2012

Shimmering like ancient crystals

Bluer than any teardrop of shame

Languid, luculent, lagoon pools

Of depth, character, purpose, aim

Flows that fleck, trickle and sparkle

Lofty ideals becoming generational

Solutions tendered, never simple

Off a duck's back – no effect at all

Until you make it your business

Pleasure, pastime go hand in hand

Between a rock and a hard place

Mirroring a world of pretend

Never pays to keep things too safe

Don't let boundaries pin you down

Better to risk your own disgrace

Or be in limbo, akimbo, aground

A lonely glance in an open field

Can at times speak volumes

Fading into the background

Until an opportunity blooms

We can all stand on the edge

Teeter tottering over the abyss

Disparity of defined decisions

A unique opaqueness occurs

But if one thing rings true

Summing up everything learned

Teacher or ardent pupil

This world can be absurd

But it grows on you

Philosophical

Abstract Alliterative Acrostalyptica
March 2014

Arguably, articulating accents accentuates addicting arousal

Beauty beseeches, burning bridges, basically brutal

Cosily coaxing, confiding, charismatically causing consent

Dabbling defenceless, drunkenly dazed, decadent descent

Exuding elegance, explicitly eager, endless elation

Fabricating fragile fables, fizzing frothily, frustration

Gracious gesticulation giving glimpses, gentle glow

Hungrily, hedonistically, hypnotically hazy, husk, hollow

Innocently invading, inspiring immersion, ironically infused

Jubilant journey, juicily jousting, jaunty jeopardy

Kindled kinship, killing kitsch, knowingly kamikaze

Lusciously laboured laughing, languishing, leisurely lingering

Majestic maestros, masking malaise, melodic mourning

Narrowly neutral, nuzzling nectar, naughtily nocturnal

Obsession, occult oration, objectified, oblique obstacle

Peculiarly pavlovian, puissant, perfectly positioned possibilities

Quixotic questing, quivering, quenching qualms quickly

Ravenously ravishing, radiating rarefied, randomised resilience

Succulent salaciousness, salvaging shimmering, sultry silence

Teasingly tempestuous temptations, torridly taking time

Undulating, unfurling, ultimately unravelling unkindness, utopian

Vigorously vociferous vessels, voicing visceral volleys

Wandering woozily with wanderlust, writhing wickedly

Xenomorphic, xenotropic, Xeroxing x-rays, xylophonic xenogamy

Yelling, yearning, yielding yourself, yesterday's yardstick

Zesty zenith, zigzagging zealously, zanily zoneless

Adios To Painful Mementos
March 2013

Travelling back in time

To a place that causes pain

All I need to get there

Is a special type of coin

What will I find through that Buffalo nickel?

Close my eyes and wish for a miracle

Taking me back, on a wayward journey

Harnessing the power of the memory

Now I'm getting in my head

A familiar sense of dread

My memories need fixing but

We're many years too late

I've stumbled back upon a dirty one

That would be better laid to rest

What kind of man would I be though

If I didn't put myself to the test

What will I find through that Buffalo nickel?

Explore my life once more, it's critical

Taking me back, back to where it all began

To a place where I was such a different man

Love had this extraordinary meaning

I had a family that I would plan

But when that all blew up in smoke

I picked up my coat and just ran

It was a couple of short years ago

Told myself I simply must let go

Lifting the curse of this fateful day

Feeling that my life had now been saved

What will I find through that Buffalo nickel?

A broken man, a record without a needle although

He became a phoenix from the ashes, he was so bold

He threw that coin into a fountain and up he rose

Stronger than before and he saw

The possibilities were endless

All he needed was a little courage

And a coin he no longer kept in his pocket

Bidding adios to painful mementos

Any Dream Will Tell You
March 2015

Looking back at the cracked mirror of my broken, bleeding heart

Slowly healing scattered pieces but there's so many scars, yet

Any dream will tell you to give it everything you've got

An ocean's waves keep pounding and its relentless exquisiteness never stops

The best and most beautiful things in the world are worth fighting for

Why should things be easy when you can embrace such perfect flaws

If you can't change direction, then why not just enjoy the ride

Our goals in life should not be just to survive but to nourish others and thrive

Spending time at night kissing the sonata of the wondrous moonlight

The stars twinkling out a symphony, bursting with orchestral delight

Smiles play out across her face, a skyline spreading infectious desire

Eyes full of romantic colours that tell so many stories filled with fire

Never limit yourself or put barriers on what you think you can do

Be the candle that spreads the light when darkness surrounds you

For if you plant the seed, you can be the tree that grows

The journey starts from within, so long as your past tragedies you can let go

Love the people that guide you and pull you back from the brink

The breath and spark of energy they provide can be more powerful than lightning

Dream of where you'll be tomorrow but build the foundations of truth today

Accept your fate, visualise the way and you'll have power to wield in your world again

No matter how slow the future starts, you're a work of art the universe needs to see unfold

Blowing The Lid Off Of This Pyramid
April 2013

When you're tempted to attempt a lie

A door opens swiftly to the other side

Slippery slope, giving yourself rope

To hang yourself out high and dry

When you go to pull the wool over

An unsuspecting victim's eyes

A deal has already been made

Confidence has been betrayed

Circumstances can otherwise dictate

The path you have decided to take

But no matter how white it all seems

Can't wash this dirt, it never gleams

Con Men and confidence tricksters

Get my knickers all up in a twist

And those Ponzi scheme guys

Can go stick it up their Sphinx

Scam artists that con old ladies

Into giving up their life savings

Put them in a boat, no sails or oars

Float into a lake full of piranhas

Nowadays, can't trust our meat or fish

Got no knowing what we could be getting

Clueless detectives with many red herrings

At least, that's what it says on the tin

So if you're going to blow smoke up

A passage where angels fear to tread

Spare a thought for whom you try to kid

Because we're all on to you now my friend

We're blowing the lid off of this pyramid

Didn't fix it properly in the first place

That's ancient Egyptian builders for you

As is often the case with real estate

Don't know what you've got until it breaks

Although to be fair they were slaves

So don't be a slave to the system

Always check the paperwork on everything

Especially when you've been drinking

The Box Rebellion
November 2012

Travelling, travailing, to an unknown destination

A speck on the cusp of an hallucinatory horizon

These thoughts are unchained, ogress beasts

Once with bewitching beauty, now pallid, gone

Swallowing whole our codifiable pigeonhole

If you fit in, you're infinitely more fathomable

Slotting together like grotesque human jenga

Demographic dictation is piquantly flavourable

Colloquially but then again not exclusively so

Membership in a club that grows and grows

Shattered, splattered, smothered, scattered

Keeping ideals means some must be thrown

Contextualised can ultimately be weaponised

Within the right reference or frame of mind

Are you truly in control of your rampant lust

When it slakes brightly behind eager eyes?

Acceleration, determination, forward at pace

Relentless, cold-hearted, a juggernaut chase

They often say you should live for the moment

So I say well then "Give me a moment's grace!"

Emerging triumphant, a view that is askance

A confident lancer leaving nothing to chance

The world you once knew is corrupted, warped

Torpidity worn as a badge in a fanciful trance

It's just a thought, a consciously lucid stream

Not really awake or even asleep it seems

We're halfway there or maybe halfway dead

Embracing the latest box ticking regime

Adjust your reverie accordingly

Breathing Stone
July 2014

Candy floss

Cotton wool mouth

Drifting off

Only to be rudely roused

Sauna in

The middle of the ocean

A clock is ticking

Mourning the morning

Fear beckons

Loss of consciousness

Dipping in and out

A toe in the water

They say that

Boredom is the only cure

Broom the witching hour fast

A pox on the night before

It will tie you up in knots

Worse than

Any boy scout or sailor

Breaking the surface

Riding the crest

Of this errant wave again

Swallow heartache

Smile in sadness

Rinse and repeat

There are no mistakes

At least none that can be seen

By the naked eye

A lock that has no key

Rusted, never to be opened

Graceful to the bitter end

Grains of perpetual sand

Unfulfilled dreams released

Into inviting arms

Welcome home, we missed you

It's never too late to change

Condimental Twins
November 2012

One goes handsomely in tandem (cha cha cha!) with the other

Sharing an intimate meal together, lovers entwined forever

To exist separately in a lonely life

That lacks the spice that we all crave

Maybe we take a little too much

A pinch here, a liberty there, in order to slake our lust

Grain by painful grain, it rubs

It's of no use crying if she makes you bitter, you indulged her

Any judge will tell you, her wealth of character inspires awe

Entertaining her as a guest, in your castle with her at the throne

You can shake it, shake it all the way down until you shiver and moan

Polar bears, frozen tundra, an icicle in the heart of a ferocious storm

Its white colour swirls like fine teardrops of snow

A pasty looking Madam, if I may be so bold to disclose

A panoply to put it mildly but bluntly, just static on a TV show

Thrown over your shoulder, she's lucky to have you, as you are her

But what of her partner, what of her non-identical twin?

To sneeze when he is breathed in

Peppered with holes, reminiscent of a toothless grin

To observe the gravy train, where one can dive in and swim

The effort worthy of the reward

It can never be said or declared

That these two are the talk of the town or are chalk and cheese

That is the nature of the beast and the bed in which they reside

Seasons they come, they go, they're upon us before we even know

These two both make a splendiferous, really cute couple though

One's strength covers the other one's weakness

A pillar to the community and a Sergeant no less

To the earth from whence they once came

That's why I encourage you to make your own

And mind your own business.

A Diverse Culture
April 2013

We brew up a storm in the Autumn shade

All of the masks that we wear, when afraid

Cast asunder from the cooking pot of shame

The leaves from the trees look on in disdain

When there is nothing left to say or sigh

A pink carnation winks its sleepy eye

And transforms into an illustrious beast

Rising high into the sky like wild yeast

When the world turns and the pot spins, spins, spins

Incorporating the many colours of your vivid dreams

Yours is an opulent ocean in a perpetual storm

Shadows ache as they twist, crawl and squirm

Serendipitously a locket curls away

Showering affection on its intended prey

Pearls of wisdom run rampant abound

Cursed in silence, at the apex they drown

Zooming in, swooping out, taciturn vociferation

Crying, stinging, triumphant prestidigitation

A fallacy to what is real and what is imagined

To dine on hope or to remain impassioned

A cornucopia of rich and tasteful exuberance

Twisting through the fog of encumbrance

Where friends become enemies and enemies friends

Light turns to dark turns to a nightmarish opaqueness

Then crash! Flashing amber blinds and subtly redefines

An ancient Indian burial ground, filled with desperate lies

Stirring the pot, emotions run rampant, they run deep

Enchanted chanting rises like the smoke from a pipe

Burying their young when their time has passed

The screams still echo, burning, yearning, aghast

But when the rain comes, we bathe in honourable shame

Of our fallen comrades, we let nature take the reins

We still have time to turn the tables on this fable

When you're the one lone voice that can't be labelled

And you call life like you have always seen it

Piece by piece, a journey that is cataclysmic

A veritable melting pot

Authentic but we're all still lost

Doctor Did Very Little For The Animals (A Dr Dolittle Spoof)
April 2014

My name's 'Doctor Did Little'

I can talk to the animals

(If by talk, you mean insult then you're on the right track)

Although, after today

Maybe I should consider

An alternative career path

The hippopotamus declared

"Does my bum look big in this?"

To wit, I replied:-

"But of course – you're a hippopotamus!"

In tears the hippopotamus

Fled straight to the owl

And the owl did scowl

With an intent to disembowel

("Doctor – there are women and children present, tone it down a tad."

"What are you, my Dad? Push off!")

I glared at the grimacing creature

Until the creepy minuscule fella

Did spontaneously combust

His feathers got in my mouth

Inconsiderate to say the least

But I guess we saved on cremation costs

Next up to try take a pop

Was a gorilla akin to King Kong

Beating his chest and waving his fists

He lunged at me with both feet first

But the sorry, hairy fool went and slipped

On an erratically placed banana skin

And fell down an open manhole cover

Into a sewer filled with shi..

(Doctor! I won't warn you again! "Sorry – moving swiftly on.")

Right about now, I thought from afar

This day couldn't get any more bizarre

When in stepped an elongated neck

Good heavens, it was a giraffe!

"Don't make me step on you man!"

He did doth threaten me with

So I took the wind out of his sails

And I promptly articulated:-

"You're having a laff, you crazy giraffe!"

"Why don't you make like a tree and leave!"

He then tried to stomp on me

Injuring his knee in the process

They tried to save him but he kept

Banging his head on the mantelpiece

So now he's pushing up the daisies

With the crispy fried owl

I suppose his friend King Kong probably drowned

Animals don't tend to last long when I'm in town

As for the sensitive hippopotamus

She'll forgive me no doubt

She asked me if she should go on a diet

I simply replied:-

"A sea food diet because when you see food….oh forget it!"

And I quietly ran off into the night

Never to darken her towels again

A Doctor's work is never done

I'm done here though, I've got a lawsuit pending

Dreaming Of Darkness Retreating
November 2014

These wings are things I must mend

If I am to fly and soar higher again

With some tender love and care

I may have a shot at banishing shame

Losing myself inside the crowd

But I'll find my way back out

The road to recovery might be long

Yet I know that I must stay strong

People obsessed with celebrating ruin

Don't have dreams worth pursuing

Everything is food for thought

Decisions have a consequence

All the freedom in the world

Means little out in the wild

When you're stranded and lacking strength

Don't be afraid to ask for help yourself

Take a chance in life, hesitate no longer

This is it and nothing more

Darkness can be beaten into submission

Make friends with fear itself for freedom

Time is scarce, words have power

Bird or prey, the choice is yours

Facing The Music
April 2014

You know my name

The way it is displayed

Blood on parched lips

Scars that seldom heal

Heartache for weeks

Drinking the homeland dry

The pain still desecrates

This is our perfect crime

Committed with practiced ease

Wiping our sleeves

On mediocrity

Ashes to ashes

Reputations to dust

Here we go again

The drama continues

Jumping from one thing

To the next

Without a care in the world

Nothing to hold us back

Feeling free but still caged

Unable to stop, to get off

From this inevitable slump

Who likes to party?

Let's do it all night

The rivers running rampantly red

A lack of restraint

Killing ourselves

One day at a time

Getting away with murder

We're our own victims

If we let the darkness in

There are no fresh starts

Or hopeful new beginnings

Redemption could be

Just around the corner yet

We feast on indulgence

Robbing life of romance

Playing a game we cannot win

Don't let excess consume everything

Friday Haikus
April 2014

Today you gave me sun

You also gave me the rain

Thanks but I'm no plant

The past is a ghost

It haunts me late in the night

Should have drank more wine

Time is limited

Please don't waste any of it

Skip mains, eat dessert

Everything you want

Is on other side of fear

What a lousy deal

Start where you are now

Use everything that you have

Conquer challenges

Ask people questions

The more random the better

Ignore their answers

Enjoy what you do

I do everything for love

Money helps too though

I ignore diets

I start with earnest but

Cake is too sexy

Music cures all ills

It nourishes me deeply

Even Death Metal

Want happy endings?

Go to movies often then

Leave before the end

Full To The Gills
September 2014

Too much to process

It's not all sinking in

I'm getting the feeling

That important items are being

Pushed out of my brain again

Information is attacking me

A series of constant streams

Facebook, Twitter, newspapers

Television, radio, YouTube

Friends conversations and magazines

Where can I find solace?

I could curl up in a warm bed

To stop the constant ringing

The banging and clanging soup kitchen

Clamouring for attention inside my head

Overstimulated late at night

Little time to sleep before light but TV cries out

The news anchor earnestly describes a murder

It haunts my tortured dreams in vivid colour

Makes me wonder why I bother watching the news any more

The sun flares up through my window

Scorching itself right up into my grill

I growl "Thrill me, day!"

No doubt, it will fail to do so

However, first I must process all my work e-mails

And abstract Picassoesque thoughts from the night before

Engrossed in my own little world, I stumble outside

To the impatiently awaiting bus up the road

Only to realise to my abject horror

I've forgotten to put on underwear

As the laughter on the bus turns to tears

I run away screaming, cursing life's twists and turns

No more multi-tasking before breakfast

I'm switching off the phone

Good riddance to communication overload

Alright, maybe just ten more posts while I eat toast

If I forget pants again tomorrow, I can always go commando

The Ghost of Poe
February 2013

Sitting yonder by the window frame, as I deeply ponder

Sleepless nights and of dreamscapes which I cannot wake

The darkness beckons me, a thick, black tar filled sea

Where forgotten realms, wispy, smoky, take lucid shape

Quicksand would be quick but this is far, far from it

Smothering, enveloping me in a vintage, accursed breath

Fighting foolishly, a ghastly, exasperating abomination

Fear, frustration and devastation strewn across my bed

Chasing danger and desire through an endless forest

Stared at by aggressive animals casting evil shadows

Snow swirling in a storm stripping me of direction

I have no choice but to soldier on and keep on going

Making sense of this peculiar nonsense slowly at first

Each piece of the puzzle falling delicately into place

Then wolves! They howl in sonorous rhythm together as
one

Aching to jump my bones and make me their helpless
victim

Through fevered illusions, I see you, tasting the blood of our love

A hazy malaise, I swallow, half-crazed, until I've eaten far too much

Snakes, rats and monsters then take turns invading my consciousness

Clamouring for attention, screaming at the top of their voices

Speaking in tongues, a myriad of guttural, quizzical languages

Pointing their paws and claws as fingers, accusatory glances

Then you pounce, a scolding ice queen banishing them away

Before turning your misguided wrath and ire, directing it at me

You murdered innocence for the sake of your own convenience

Slaked your own lust at the expense of another's feelings

So now it's inside the walls of my mind where you will reside

Brick by painful brick, I've blocked you off and left you to die

At times I wonder, sitting despondently, if I have been possessed

Does the Ghost of Poe and his visions reside within my reluctant chest?

Will I ever shake off the shackles of this nightmarish experience?

Will I ever be able to yearn, to burn, to find true love again?

Or will I sink without a trace, deep into this darkness?

I would ask a raven or a cat but they would not answer back

But I now have faith in love, it's not the nightmare it once was

Finding solace in prose and comfort in elegant, gorgeous words

So I'll use them to create worlds and make ours a better place

Banishing the pain and suffering that you helped to create

The Ghost of Poe has taught me that I really should let go

And with it my nightmares will pale and no longer haunt me so

Forever more

Give Me A Little Danger Of My Own, Stranger
July 2014

I don't know who you are

I've admired you from afar though

Through curtain cracks, empty shop doorways

And abandoned railway parking lots

You come across as quite extraordinary

The way you move and glide is like

An elegant swan or a frolicking gazelle

Whether you're tying your shoelace

Or falling down an open manhole

You're poetry in motion to be sure

I think I am falling madly in love with you

From your great big bulbous head

All the way down to

Your hairy Neanderthal toes

Some may scream at your hideous visage

I just think that you are simply remarkable

But I'm getting ahead of myself

I really should start this letter more formally

So, let me begin with Dear Sir or Madam

I afraid I can't be more specific

Because you're blurry and too far away

Is that a fetching hat or a bad haircut?

Tomorrow's agenda – get my eyesight checked

Also since we've only met in my mind

I really don't think I'm qualified

To form a rational opinion

So I will finish by saying

"Will you be mine?"

P.S. Feel free to write me a letter in reply

Oh, you did? Why thank you, so kind

Wait a minute, this is a restraining order

I thought we had something together

Guess you can't judge a book by its cover

Stranger Danger! I'll never talk to them again

At least, not in this zoo or in this lifetime

A Hobby The Whole Family Can Enjoy
April 2014

I like me, I really do

Yet sometimes

I feel like I need

To scream my head clean off

Just to feel the release

It's hard to laugh in the world today

When your only true friend is money

No more faults than the average person

Mediocrity still carries a perpetual burden

Sincerity may be the one thing to slow you down

For me it's the only currency in town

Push me aside rather than create a scene

Let's feast upon these uneasy feelings

Hiding in our shells, timid turtles

Afraid to take a stand for what's right

The boss at home, it must be said though

Fiefdom comes at a terrible price

In an age that is more digital than physical

Where relationships can often

Be erased and replaced

I'm inclined to take my own personal view

Why can't we work harder in the first place?

What's important in life

Is the strength of connections

Everyone should be allowed

To give strangers the option

If they won't play along

Don't hesitate to ditch them

A hobby the whole family can enjoy

Better to create than destroy

Leaky Bucket
December 2012

Furtively it glances, as it crosses the room

Marking its territory as it grows, blooms

Fearful of knocking anything useful over

A symptom of the chaos and disorder

To touch it, experience the warm embrace

Protecting it, shielding it like a carapace

Mind and body entwined as one entity

Accepting the violence of the generosity

But like all moments that are fleeting, fleeing

You hold on for dear life, pleading, beseeching

Dancing in a decadent waltz until you fall

Alone in the darkness, pallidly mauled

The journey is there but the essence escaped

Genie left the bottle, destruction in his wake

Where is your sanity, where is your map?

Lost at sea then boom! A thunderous clap

They say lightning never strikes twice

Looking at this gift horse right in the mouth

Precisely planned, hell – how could you miss?

With infallible accuracy, a little to the left

Taking another sweep, gesticulating wildly

Will it stop this time and behave less badly?

Strained pink sieve, permeable membrane

Hoping that it sticks, goes against the grain

Capture and preservation is the key

Collecting and tagging your errant butterfly

Putting an original stamp on this world

Allowing the talent to unfurl, to uncurl

Chasing rainbows before they disappear

Colours run red, dry, black, misty, unclear

Clarity can ultimately become your friend

If you understand how your universe bends

Caressing the shape, tasting the jagged thrill

Fast or slow, its core molten, fundamental

A mantra for this day and age it seems

It's a gift that doesn't cost a thing

I guess it's up to you how you use it

The nuances, textures, nuggets

And how you go about plugging

Your leaky bucket…no, again you've lost it

Slippery little devil

Left Logically Yet Rightly Creative
November 2014

Basements are where we find ourselves, if we want to retreat from an indifferent world

Consolation comes alongside an axe to grind, since everyday life expects us to experience and overcome lows

Curtains are certain to come down on individuals, if their unsavoury motives are summarily revealed

Denial of ideals means we can't connect to those we care about to see how good we make them feel

Expectations are always too high; demands we foist upon us just to impress others are unreasonable

Jittering from one thing to the next leads to unnecessary stress, the effects are often irreversible

Masks cannot help but slip when there's nothing for them to grip; they soon start feeling fake

Obituaries are read side by side a heavy heart, the death of any relationship ultimately has tolls to pay

Restless in our endeavours, we're repeatedly trying to please too many bodies with meagre time, all at once

Shivers run up and down our spines, whether we create them out of either fear or excitement

Swaying to the music when it fizzles in our minds, a defence mechanism designed to slay boredom

Swollen eyes from staying up round the clock, striving to finish off things we passionately believe in

Tumbling in headfirst isn't the best strategy, unless you enjoy being hurt right from the start

Whiskey provides us a fiery kick but if you don't like it then any alcohol or sugar rush will work

Meanwhile, on the other hand and flipside of this yin and yang coin

There are tons of cool things down here, silence allows us to focus consciousness in the **Basement**

Is it such a bad thing if we encounter lows? There wouldn't be highs otherwise if it's any **Consolation**

Trust is in short supply, it pays to keep our minds open wide, we must draw open the **Curtains**

Lauding ideals as pinnacles of evolution is what we strive for, no more living in the shadow of **Denial**

Playing to our strengths has consequence of giving everything our best, so we can raise **Expectations**

Questions we must ask, why are we are we so restless, then fix at the source to avoid **Jittering**

Hiding in obscurity just to please someone else? If we maintain our true identities, no need for any **Masks**

Relationships can die but teach us how to live and love stronger than before, new beginnings not **Obituaries**

A perfectionist is fine but you can't please everyone all of the time, so be calm and less **Restless**

Abandon fears and instead, deliver pleasure to your lover, spine tingling affection creating **Shivers**

Music is soul nourishment, breathing in every note and word, mountains moved, opinions are now **Swaying**

Cheeks should be engorged from copious smiling and laughing, whereas egos should never ever be **Swollen**

Pride usually arrives before a fall but we don't tend to learn anything, unless at first we're **Tumbling**

Everybody has a shot at a happy life, true love and laughter, so in honour, let's raise a toast with a glass of **Whiskey**

In the end, maybe we all just want the same thing

If we help each other, there's nothing we can't accomplish

Let's Call It A Day
December 2012

Taking bold risks on some bad eggs

Finding yourself back on the shelf

And now you're fighting below the belt

Digitized, dangerously displayed

Ornamentally organised but caged

Fragments of antiquated truth still remain

Settling into a motley groove

Nothing left to prove, pursue

No choice left but to let yourself cut loose

Cogs turn through this wizened life

The way the wheel turns is divine

Water spilled as precious as if it were wine

Dilated, pupated anachronisms

Syrupy, serendipitous dreams

From page to mouth via expressionism

Dulled senses, potent sedative

Censored, rough edges edited

Picturesque, a suitably macabre postcard

Controversial decisions

Sensations or experience

Balance your brilliance, distil your essence

Holding firm, resolute or absolute

Entropy can't be the only route

A paradoxical farce with but one use

Play the game, find the clues

Intrepid explorers on the move

Intimidated by a Machiavellian world

Why not keep all things simple?

Refrain from becoming medieval

Engineering engorgement on general principle

Concordant conjecture

Dominates social media

Until we're all courting disaster

Convenient or expedient

A lover's incorrigible lament

The future harshly judging the present

So we navigate with a swing

Shadows cast, a bell rings

Exotic yet disintegrating

Linear right from the beginning

The Lies We Tell Our Children
January 2013

Son, pick yourself up off that floor

Stop folding yourself like a concertina

We didn't raise you to be a ballerina

Or have a spine like a faulty deck chair

Ragdoll floppiness, tantrums thrown

Means no sweets, toys, none of those

As for you yelling that horrible scream

Ice cream is fast becoming a pipe dream

Your budgie died and went to heaven

He's not sitting in a hole in the ground

Buried him to give him brand new angel wings

Now he flies through dirt, concrete, everything

Eat your greens, broccoli makes you taller

Just take a look at your Father

Now, I know he's only five foot six

That's because he eats too many biscuits

"Are we there yet?" just a little further

That's what I told you and your sister

Pretty much about ten miles ago

But when Daddy's lost, just go with the flow

You'll get it next time we're in the shop

I left my purse in the car glove compartment

If I've got no money, why am I buying wine?

You'll understand in thirty years' time

Yes, I know I called you a miniature terrorist

To be fair they're far easier to reason with

So if you don't behave right now

You leave me with no choice

To call the police and have you

Thrown to the wolves

What's that, you promise you'll be good?

Well then, that's great, I love you too

Ain't that the truth!

Made Whole Again
Jan 2015

A puzzle is forming with precision,

its pieces unknown

Past echoes linger,

basking under the shadow

Of an unforgiving frozen sun

Estranged from a life

that ravenously thrives on change

Overwhelming a natural need

to be made whole again

Loss can cause us to want to forget

the special moments that were once shared

Sacrificing humanity

we become empty and scared

Yet by reminding ourselves we're human,

to cherish all things

we can pull ourselves back from the brink

Outrageous courage should flourish

and be maintained at all times

Uncluttering our purpose

A singular vision begins to unfold

The concept no longer alien,

foreign, forbidden, fictional

We're conquering new ground

breaking all the moulds

The more mysterious and bizarre

the situation is

The more our strength of character

should be used to dispel all evils

For we must fill the void

with sincerity, generosity and hope

Only then will we know which path to choose

No longer a faceless entity

Made whole again by love's gentle touch

A Monster Of A Story
April 2014

An aberration, the shape of bulging glass

Unwelcome, steroidal bulk of a figure

Looming aggressively in the shadows, alone

A school bully expelled from the classroom

Dynamic, dramatic, silvery spine

Arrow slit eyes add depth and character

Drab grey totem pole face

Stitched back together the wrong way

Frankenstein in a melting, lumpen shell

Clawing at his inflated, purple back

Flies swarm to this compost heap

A visual nightmare for the senses

Silhouettes choked, all knotted, sinuous blobs

Shakespeare's quills could not imagine

Sinister black and white stripes bursting

Across gaudy porcelain, midnight blue skies

An accidental nod to ugly, angular pinstripes

Painful proof that the fight has now been lost

Not content with an assortment of bloodlust

He turns on you, planning the extent of his wrath

Pushing, gnawing, twisting you to the broken cliff-face

The skies scorched with chaos and death

A forest of sticks and stumps

Knuckledusters punching at unforgiving air

Stubbed out like a cigarette, you tumble

Taking him with you though to the ocean below

Cast adrift, a piece that has lost its way

At peace now though, in a watery grave

A dubious accolade but the monster now slayed

Remembering not the beast but the battle itself

A New Beginning
April 2014

My bones are made of stone

The streets are paved with gold

As I follow this winding road

The mystery begins to unfold

Rushing to touch a majestic sky

Watching it seethe, roar and sigh

Landmarks hauntingly familiar

Have now just simply disappeared

Wondering whether I should descend

Can't see anyone for miles around

Trying to fathom the rhyme or reason

Why I am stuck in this barren prison

Stumbling blindly to the precipice edge

How long have I been here? Days? Months?

It all looks so peaceful, so eerily serene

I am gazing at a beautiful oil painting

This place has seduced me and confused me

I am not sure that I will ever leave

Yet if I am to win this endless race

I need to understand myself

To discover who I really am

Before I step into oblivion

Perhaps I am bound on this path

Blazing a trail for others to follow

A shallow folly full of misinterpretation

History trailing in its wake behind me

There must be a hole

In the bottom of this boat

Perhaps I should walk

On the surface of the lake

Wave goodbye to those

Whose outlines have blurred

Unable to make their escape

Still, I must wander on

For a few more miles

It is my truth, my curse, my burden

I have looked deep into the mountains

Therein lies my salvation

The sun setting on a new beginning

But first, I must rest a while

These bones are wet and tired

Funny because it hasn't been raining

They were once warm, now coldness is spreading

Creeping like an animal, I must rest on the wall

A false dawn awaits, through tears I blink

I dream of you and us sitting at the lake

I will find you soon my love

Although seductive sleep takes hold

Know that I will be there soon

In a place of shadows and rain we call home

Searching For Release
April 2014

Tempus fugit

Time flies

Scattered raindrops

Flowing through my mind

This wall of fog

I climb and I climb

Keep fighting and falling

An endless pantomime

I'm tempted

To be a fugitive

I'm wandering days

Not knowing what I will find

Now I know for certain

That's it's curtains

I've seen the signs

Tempus fugit

Time flies

It is but a metaphor for the mind

Whispering endlessly

Searching for release

A place to deal with all the truth and lies

Tempus fugit

Time flies

Can't stop the flow

All I can do is just follow

I'm a slave to the beat

I do my best to cope but

At times it hurts just to exist

Social Accountability
April 2014

Social media, you tricked us all good

An imposter as to what you have to offer

It all started out as just information

Sharing is caring you said

Now it's all gunning for LOL's

Funny accidents and amusing cat pictures

Late at night, we're getting intimate

I'm losing sleep and I can't stop

You chew me up and then you spit me out

An entertainment junkie can't get enough

What celebrity do I look like this week?

Let's fire up the Comparison Application

I got Channing Tatum of course

I can see the resemblance

Except my six pack is missing

Plus, I'm not even American

Facebook, Twitter or let me Instagram it

A memory for us all to cherish

Though at the time I was drunk

Those people I was with, I don't know their names

Also, I'm pretty sure that's illegal in seven States

And possibly nine countries

Let's take another random quiz

Am I an animal, a book, a car?

A malevolent dictator, a faded superstar?

Perhaps a type of frog or an Indian raindance?

I'm slowly struggling with my identity

Last night I worked out what brand I would be

If I was a packet of frozen peas

No time to lament about things

Before the internet would be better left unsaid

The messages have gone viral as videos

Across flaming YouTube channels and Vimeo

Now there's a price on your head

Guess there is nothing we can do

Except strap ourselves in for the ride

It's all or nothing if you're saying anything

So delete all your profiles

Or be prepared to suffer the consequences

Glorious or tragic

They're all good for a laugh

Just don't expect your lives to remain private

That kind of thing remains in the past

Unreliable Witness
April 2013

Do you wear glasses, even if it's just to read?

Your eyesight is clearly failing

You're exactly what my client needs

Can I interest you in a bribe?

I assure you we will be discreet

We don't want this to blow up in your face

How good are you at keeping secrets?

Around a variety of dodgy issues?

Glad to hear your moral compass is turned off!

You see the thing about scruples is

There's no room for them in modern business

At least where there's money involved

Can I tempt you with our 2 for 1 deal?

We will supply you with a disguise

A fake identity will be supplied

You'll earn frequent flyer miles

And 10% off restaurant meals

On Sundays, if you book online

We've gone over your testimony

Particularly the gaps in your memory

Everything seems to be just fine

Your credibility will be reduced

Gradually at first then all at once

Just remember, it's a series of white lies

We'll give you a wink, a nudge and a cough

That will be your cue for a great performance

Keep the theatrics nice and simple enough

Then when your done and the dust has settled

The cheque will be sent out in the mail

A nice tidy sum made payable

Don't spend it all at once however

We may need a scapegoa...er...an alibi later

And your name's on the invoice letter!

Pleasure doing business with ya (sucker)

Vintage Dangers
April 2014/

Exploring ancestral roots

Baring our teeth

Resurrected in sound

Celebrating death

DIG

DON'T QUESTION IT

Climatic signs

Vying for hungry eyes

Pictures painted backward

Stealing all the smiles

KEEP DIGGING

THE JOY IS IN THE GIVING

Voyaging out to sea

Portraying a thief

No crocodile tears shed

Dining on vintage release

GETTING CLOSER

IT'S ALMOST OVER

The heart starts beating

All thoughts merely fleeting

Controversial secrets found

Better left eternally sleeping

JUST A BIT MORE

KNOCKING AT THE DOOR

Sharing words with those you love

With everyone you grew up around

A bunch of letters, photos, unanswered questions

The past should remain buried underground

YOU'VE ARRIVED

INNOCENCE LOST

Because once you start, you cannot stop

You can never go back

Death maybe the enemy of humanity

But family endures and stubbornly lives on

This is the danger of nostalgia

Particularly if we're talking about

That nude photo of me

At the beach when I was twelve

I thought I burned them all

Those magnificent buns refuse to go down

Whoppers
April 2014

The earth is round? Nope

It's flatter than a strawberry pancake

Around the world in 80 days?

I can do it in one on roller skates

The sun is not much hotter

Than my radiator on all day at full blast

The moon needs to stop poking his nose

Into other people's business

Knitting needles make

Superbly cheap antennas for dogs

Empty cigarette packets are ideal carrying cases

For frogs (with smoker's coughs)

String is an excellent alternative

For barbed wire, if you wrap it many times

Used tea bags can be dried outside

And fashioned into beautiful hats and handbags

You can easily lose weight

If the only thing you ever eat is cakes

Also, raisin based cookies taste identical

To the ones smothered with chocolate chips

Birthdays can be tons more fun

If you only invite rich people to them

Every gift must be a yacht

You can always learn to swim afterwards

No man has ever been shot

As he is doing the dishes

Then again no man has ever done them

In the first place (cue angry men comments)

Fast is better than slow

Both in the boardroom and bedroom

In, out and put the kettle on

Not my motto but feel free to make it your own

And then I'll have to disown you

That's not how I roll

Love/Romance

14 Words For Love – The Definitive Collection
February 2015

You never fail to impress

Stunning and delicious

In your dress made of tortillas

You hold key to my heart

But your Mother nags

She's superglued the lock

No boundaries here

Falling completely for somebody is scary

But gratifying in the extreme

A kiss is nature's way

Of exploring delicious terrain

Stalactites and stalagmites

Mouth tennis

Aphrodite

Everything you do makes me weak in the knees

Even brushing your teeth

Sipping chilled wine

Holdings hands, appreciating golden sunsets

Misty eyed

Choking on a vol-au-vent

Love has a noble purpose

It allows us to forgive quirks

And embrace uniqueness

When you're around

Senses are heightened

Touch, smell, taste

And also nonsense, I'm besotted

Getting lost in your eyes

Could swim there forever

Or at least until breakfast

I married myself

Got me a wedding gift

It is a very nice wig

Ambrosial Moments
October 2014

Under the wickedly salacious lust spell

Cast by the shadow of the crescent moon

A passionate embrace takes place in a raging ocean

Of wine soaked words whispered all night long

These twilight hours seem so serenely peaceful

You are such a rose between two thorns

I cannot help but to feel connected to you

You cause shivers from my spine deep into my soul

From daybreak's first light, peeking out from the covers

When you're near, summer sun never seems to set

Held prisoner by your gaze and smile, capturing my heart

You steal my breath away and then your kisses give it
back

In all of the ambrosial moments that we've spent together

Mutual pleasure has made us burn brighter than the stars

On a slow ride to heaven, there's no stopping this train

So happy and exhilarating that we're the only passengers

Dreamy tunes whistle from a tangy, sensual breeze

Hands so soft and delicate, as we caress then squeeze

A special bond formed from precious bouts of tenderness

Forever lost in each other and each other's dreams

When a spark as strong as this ignites torrid flames

There can be no other outcome or course of action

We must surrender to our most basic, animalistic instincts and urges

Celebrate the alignment of the earth, moon, sun, stars and nature

Bathe in the inherent beauty, mystery, sensuality, awe and wonder

Letting the universe decide how this parable ultimately unfolds

Better to be engulfed in love's warmth than be left out in the cold

For if heaven forbid, the fire's embers were to inadvertedly wane

A life lived pursuing true love

Is a fulfilling existence truly worth living

Chasing Her Eclipse
April 2015

Convicted we could be

Of playing our chosen tune

How sordid are life's demands

The world will have its own

I may take this promise

Your Servant will become a King

The Queen will teach me paradise

With lips of earnest flames

I would never let her go

Leaping close to her side like

A possessed squirrel

Although, a flower deserves a preferred path

Akin to a saucer holding a cup

Chasing the eclipse has taught me

Not to dwell on the minutiae

But they say that dust sticks

Even if the pebble is pushed away

Would you play Hide & Seek

If you knew the surgeon will not come

This might have been the hand

That smoothed a homely pain

It is sweeter to obey

Than to chase the bee with the honey

But bear the brunt of this errand

And know a tree may ultimately blossom

To teach you a lesson

That everyone has a chance

Even the smallest citizen

If you use your loaf

And make that promise to her in advance

Feasting On Feral Feelings
February 2013

She could pounce like a tiger, a cougar on the range

When she digs her claws in, it's impossible to escape

Feels like I'm jumping with no parachute, into the sea

Sinking to the bottom of an ethereal, underwater city

If I make the mistake of letting her through the door

Cannot fake euphoria, I'm on the floor begging for more

A delicious, burlesque carnival of carnality begins

Her glamour is much greater than a shower of diamonds

Sweeter than any fruit plucked from a blossoming tree

I'm drunk on her tune, she croons it oh so softly

Floating on a bubble of champagne mixed with fun

Romance electrifies the air, two hearts beating as one

She's sending me messages, a veritable network of signals

Broadcasting winks, nods, nudges on salacious channels

You can fight her if you dare and at your own peril

But if she finds you unprepared, your feelings will go feral

Creatures of the night when we embrace our passions

Wild beasts conviving in intoxicating abandonment

When we're holding the world in the palm of our hand

Nothing seems impossible, nothing seems to taste bland

Finding the maps to navigate these uncharted waters

An arrow leads the way, heading straight right for us

When it pierces us deep, stroking our amorous cores

The volcanic desire erupts and there are no survivors

We are heading on a journey of discovery and destiny

The more we learn about each other, the greater the intensity

Celebrating each and every day as if it were ornate treasure

The pleasures of the flesh, there can be nothing finer

So grab your partner, some candy and some gorgeous flowers

Scented candles and oils, an aromatically powerful balance

Sensually indulge senses, true feelings, let your love grow

Leave those dirty dishes until you've finished tomorrow

And if you're single and can't get physical

Curl up with a book, film, wine, nice meal

Treat yourself like a king or a queen

And let's raise a glass to next time

A Felicitous Word
January 2014

A wish made on someone, in summer years ago

Face scrunched up, sparkling eyes, a beautiful nose

Simple things that go unnoticed by the world

I could never forget the virtue of this girl

Keeping an old picture of her in my wallet

Private comments made us silent for a moment

Wrapped her up in a flurry of hugs and kisses

Holding hands like normal people, as always

No song could match our important first date

Memories tattooed in gold you couldn't erase

Celebrate small things, including the beginning

Humanity is a gift that is a part of living

That newspaper and the number written inside

Stories so heavy, threaded, surviving time

Different man, safe location, a holiday with no names

Sat down happily by each other on the living room couch for days

We exist and then tomorrow is cut off

"Remember!" they said, all foggy, militant

It was a misted, colourless picture

The smile in their eyes years ago as they once were

This is why we made a long list

So we could dance in the light of the moon

In the event of a big deal or situation

Family celebration is magical at fixing all that is wrong

Doctor, teacher or philosophical leader

They will all tell you the same

Everywhere changed

And no-one breathed a felicitous word

Finding The Paradox
April 2015

Not sure how much my heart can hold

Kisses stolen like there is no tomorrow

In the beginning, a flame arose

An outlet required for it to evolve

Finding the paradox once and for all

Offering a slow, sensual dance as it unfolds

The only reality is that circumstances change

Waves, the tides turning, nothing stays the same

Touch is a source that constantly restores existence

The world can be such a hard habit to break

Learning by paying attention, whatever the stakes

Smallest details can make the biggest difference

It is easy to hate how things may not work out

Future's not written but the past is just words

Speak with a fierce integrity and you will find

Everyone should have positive influences in their life

And in the end, if flames anew flare into a fire

With hope becoming a replacement for fear

Let's be optimistic and see this through

Give yourself generously without fail

Keep your heart and mind wide open

Only then will you be ready for the right person

Hot Little Biscuit
November 2014

No point in putting make-up on because it will melt clean off

Your face is a waffle iron grill with the dial set to argh!

There's a longing in my loins that desperately needs to be girded

All the fire hydrants you just passed by have now exploded

Are those cargo pants, skinny jeans or trousers that you're wearing?

To be honest you could wear a potato sack and I'd still be salivating

These emotions that we're experiencing are really quite revealing

Let's dance dirtily right after I've peeled my lusty self off of the ceiling

You're my hot little biscuit

I've got no choice but to dunk it

Come rain or shine, there's always room

For a bit of gravy on the side, alright?

The wheels and rims you're displaying are unquestionably satanic

Turning and burning while I'm yearning for something idiosyncratic

All these crumbs of sin are finding their way in, heading down to Chinatown

You always know how to push my buttons, especially the forbidden ones

If you can't stand the heat, then you shouldn't frequent kitchens

Firing off on all cylinders is all well and good when nobody is looking

Actions speak louder than words when you're setting fireworks off in mouths

We've bitten off more than we can chew but it's too late to spit it out

You're my hot little biscuit

Taking afternoon tea to extremes

With you I can be anyone, I can be almost anything

Baby, you're an excess of sugar in my bloodstream

You're my hot little biscuit

A blessing in disguise

When I take you out on a whim for a spin

Delicious chaos ensues every time

No smoke without fire but I choose to smoke only bacon and fools

Giving me all the right saucy, chutzpah moves to take you seriously like typhoons

A rush of blood going straight to our heads, blowing us both to smithereens

I know I can count on you to be discrete until the paparazzi comes calling

You're my hot little biscuit

There's no point beating about the bush

If you're not the one for me

No point crying over spilt milk

But you're my hot little biscuit

Full of sass, spice and award winning ingredients

Let's celebrate this sensually unholy union

No matter what the risks

It takes two to tango with the devil

Yet it only takes one bite to go up in flames

We'll put them out with champagne

Whoops, we've fanned the fires again

Why are my mistakes just so damn sexy?

Reciprocation of sticky situations

Personality always goes such a long way

We'll leave the rest up to gravity

Hot Or Cold, You're Gold
April 2014

Give me a little sugar

To make the time fly by right

Pour it right into me

Why not keep me up all night?

I'll take you hot or cold

These lips wrap around so tight

You're all natural

I'm lost just after one bite

I often feel like a slave

When you dig your claws firmly in

I try to resist your wily ways

Yet the temptation is far too strong

I'll take you with some coffee

We'll down a few liquors

Perhaps a slice of cake

You complement everything of course

Some say you're so gothicly dark

With a power so rampantly raw

If they let you in and you engulf them

They can't cope with your fatal flaws

I say to hell with it

Throwing caution to the wind

Tomorrow the guilt may overwhelming

But tonight we'll indulge in sin

Devouring each other

Until there is nothing left

You speak a language in my ear

Whispered without a shadow of doubt

You're candy to me, my dear

You melt in my mouth

The Ice Maiden
April 2014

I'd go nuts over you

Skin sweeter than sugar

You're anything but plain vanilla

So cool, you make me shiver

Our relationship started

On a rocky road

Until you became minted

I fell head over heels

Your curves rocked my world

Raising me from my troubles

We'll go for coffee afterwards

Around you, all my entendres double

No-one could split us like bananas

Peeking at nothing but the skyline

Buttering each other up

Smooth as purest silk

It is often that I find you

Naked as the day you were born

I wrap myself in a passionate embrace

Loving how you melt beneath my touch

I've tried all the flavours

Everything you could possibly imagine

I've been to Paris, Rome, to Amsterdam

And that one with four R's in

That no-one understands

But in the end, my good lady

You're the only one for me

Almost bohemian

Honeycombed hair in your pretty face

With a hint of chocolate freckles

Oh, Ice Maiden, that's how I ravish thee

From the fridge then back home to my belly

Just A Phase We're Going Through
November 2012

A grin made of cheese

Lovers dance beneath

Its luminescent gaze

Fragile thoughts, across the surface

Strong of arm, steps and leaps of purpose

Cavernous conundrum

Wind swept crater

We all need our space

At one time or the other

When we land on our feet

Might as well be butter side up

Howling like ancient wolves

The need to feed consumes us

Bonds are forged on nights like these

Whispered in ears, surreptitious thieves

Scholars, scientists, artists, explorers

Illuminating all of life's shadowy corners

Naked eye eclipsed, a perspective mangled

A cycle that is spherically entangled

Getting caught in a whirlwind of time

Leaning heavily on a burdened brain

Smiles as big as crescent canyons

But no atmosphere/companions

Raw ingredients, knocked-off chemistry

A blustery, illustrious kind of bombastry

Slowly beginning to reveal its secrets

Until you've had your fill at nights

Now it's over, you're feeling blue

Not a miracle, we just decided to go

A symbol that all of our hearts knew

Just a phase we're going through

There's always time to embrace something anew

The Kitten Of Compassion
April 2014

Love is the wildest, most unpredictable thief on the planet

It either nourishes your soul or tears you clean in two

Sounds heavenly, tastes divine, touches sensuously

Its hungry look can slay in an instant

Its smell raising hell between the satin sheets

I feel it in the air, colours seem more vivid

Triggering passion in my bones whenever you're around

I see it in the words you use and your tone of voice

You're more majestic than Queen Elizabeth of Buckingham Palace

(As you can no doubt tell, I'm British)

I said it was unpredictable

Yet sometimes it can be quite plain and simple

Uninvited, unrequited, unbearable yet still welcome

I don't know what it's doing half the bleeding time

Horses for courses I suppose

I hunger for more each day even when I'm full

Doesn't matter where I am in equilibrium

On the demand/supply curve of this kingdom

I'm still an affectionate kitten of compassion

I yearn for a heart not cold as forged marble

That speaks to me softly as it beats, an orchestral marvel

Fuelling my ascent, taking us both to the heavens

Davey Crockett right here respects people and their emotions

I can see that one day dreams will come true

That guided by a nourishing light of mutual companionship

Each day takes on a more desirable and engaging hue

Of course not all people are at risk, some are even immune

I'm certainly not one of those though by any shape or opinion

A buoyant pancake on the great steaming grill pan of life

I know that if I keep fighting and don't stop for one second

Even if it's to catch my breath, I'll still keep on going strong

Until I hear the sirens and the paramedics, whoops, a bit too long!

Let me start again when my blue lips go red again

As I utter the immortal words "Gato con guantes no caza ratones"

(A cat with mittens cannot hunt mice)

I must launch myself headfirst full of dedication and courage

I am reminded of Puss In Boots and his wonderful eyes, as he said

"My thirst for adventure will never be quenched!"

I'll leave the door unlocked this time

And my heart on display in an ornate glass case

I'll be waiting

Let Your Heart Be Your Guide
October 2014

Romance can change people

Broadening perspectives in life

Opening up the mind's eye

To an epiphany of possibilities

Romance can heal the world

Spreading happiness, true love and hope

It can inspire freedom of choice

Giving us our own seductive, individual voice

Romance can colour our dreams

Optimistically enhancing self-esteem

Making every day a birthday

Mellifluous moments where songs are always playing

Romance can make a difference

No matter what the trial or tribulation

If we treat love and people with respect

We can all experience perfect relationships

Be kind, caring, compassionate and considerate

And above all, always let your heart be your guide

A Lightning Bolt To The Heart
April 2014

They say nice guys finish last

Why does everything have to be a race?

If I want to hold open doors, buy flowers

Pay women compliments for their endeavours

It shouldn't be considered a disgrace

Being courteous is not a weakness

I don't want to be cheap or fake

The power of listening closely to opinions

Giving advice straight from the heart

A lightning bolt to the senses in the confidence stakes

If there's one thing that I hold dear

It is the determination to be sincere

I hold on to this value for dear life

It is my mantra that defines myself

It's what keeps me going despite impossible odds

Maybe I come from a different time and place

My romantic ideals seem a million miles away

Yet to give is to receive far more potently

Never getting old, always better in each and every way

The exuberance of the process I enjoy to this very day

So what if I come across as quaint?

A relic from some forgotten past

I proudly wear my emotions out in the open

Wounding easily but still healing quickly when broken

A friend to those who want me to embrace them

I'll be your shoulder to cry on, to the bitter end

The one that doesn't give up, whatever the cost

In this perfect moment, all we have to do is look back

We've achieved so much together on this journey

Time to reflect and finish what we started

Your glance and your touch could move mountains

Where we both go next is an adventure in the making

To treat you well is a choice well worth taking

Making It Out Alive
October 2014

Afraid to lose control of this volatile world

Everything feels fake when it should feel real

It's like someone has broken the handle off

Finding myself washed up on the shores of hell

Wasting my breath, paying good lip service

Thinking with my heart instead of my head

People say if it's easy, it's just not worth pursuing

This gloriously, gorgeously confounding thing called love

An ending is still a brand new beginning

Death gives birth to alternative paths

If we embrace light over the accursed darkness

Things might turn out differently at last

Sometimes we struggle

To maintain our own unique edge

We let it get swallowed

Time and again, ad infinitum

Turning our backs on our own strengths

Losing the thread of who we truly are

Don't deny your dreams and your sense of purpose

Let them rise to the surface without delay

Adoration and passion

Should fill everything that you do

Fear should never come into play

Lions we roar, with each shout it becomes clear

Pushing ourselves to the core of our limits

We're not going down without a fight

We'll find our way back, make no mistake

Letting love colour our ravenous hearts

No matter how complicated it gets

We'll make it out of this thing alive

I need to lose myself in you tonight

Making Sense Of Love
April 2014

Touch me

Tell me how it feels

When I stroke your delicate face

Your presence intoxicates

Breathing you in through everything

And it feels like home

Taste me

All over your wicked tongue

We've never done it

This way before

I can't help thinking

Déjà vu is just around the corner

Look at me

Drink in every single drop

Finer than wine that is exquisite

I savour every moment

As if this were the last

Temptation on this earth

Listen, can't you hear?

Our heartbeats pounding as one

The rhythm on a mission

Adrenaline rushing us with no hope

Or desire to slow this thing down

In passion's flames we drown now

Give me your hand

You will be my ruin

Your smile is enough to finish me off

Yet your tender kiss brings me back to life

Why is love so complicated?

When a spark to the senses

Is all that you need

What a glorious way to die

Touch, taste, smell, sound and sight

Now the puzzle is complete

Naked As The Sun
December 2014

A storm brews ominously from within,

rumbling beneath anxious, pulsating veins

Lurking, bubbling, it writhes,

hungry for action, hotwiring synapses in my mind

Reminding me of muscle memory,

bones infused with ancestral coping techniques

Caverns where once complete darkness was a thief,

now radiate only fiery light

Any vestige remaining of a harrowing past

is replaced with prestige of the future

Finding redemption lies in the heart

of leaving behind things making you bitter

For all of the lines that we draw in the sand,

defining each of us as woman or man

If we cross them without caution,

we can be left exposed, as naked as the sun

Giving up your mind, body and soul

to rapture's tenderly romantic yet greedy embrace

Rampant consumption is quite common

when it's all or nothing, whatever the stakes

A liar to yourself if you don't appreciate

that devotion takes a significant toll

Although every gesture is a raw revival

of exhilaration, intoxication, it enthrals

When you lose yourself to the noise,

succumbing to the seductive beat from inside

Take care, don't forget,

you're a person with feelings and goals in your own right

Nothing is more charming than who you are

or fighting for what you believe in

Be selfless in your acts of compassion

people won't see a defenceless person

Love's bond becomes stronger

with passion and dedication, it can never be broken

The Only Light That Matters In My World
April 2014

You are important to me

You always have been

When you're not there

A massive hole presents itself

I'm no longer in control of my world

Your devilish grin lights up

The whole room we're in

Every inch of darkness

Banished, as your beauty blossoms

Radiating purity like there's no tomorrow

Your feelings mean something

They carry weight in ways

That are difficult for those

On the outside looking in

To fully comprehend and understand

The lengths I would go to for you

Your voice makes a difference

Whatever you have to say

The words spill out harmoniously

All warm, honey-coated and glazed

You could read the phone book all day

I would still be in awe and infatuated

Your story has substance

From the whole thing

To something so simple

Like where you come from

What you ate for breakfast

To what's been bugging you today

Every little detail is magical in its own way

Your life is all that matters to me

To help you on your path

Is the greatest privilege

In which I can partake

Your friends, your family, all of us

Colour each picture of our journey

I take pleasure in painting this epic portrait

Keep on knowing that I always will

Be there for you in heart, spirit, adventure and thrills

You're the only light I've ever known

The only light that can be seen in my world

From now until the end of time

The Path That Lies Ahead
June 2014

Soft gossamer clouds

Smooth as creamiest silk

Converging on to a barren shore

Worlds emerge and collide

A prophesy unfolds and unwinds

The mystery is stirring

In an ancient land

Time has once forsaken

Two lovers spending an eternity

Lost in each other's twinkling eyes

Holding eager, wandering hands

A fizzy cocktail of devotion

Consummate immersion

Across a windswept, unkempt

Yet hauntingly beautiful horizon

The path that lies ahead

Both romantic and obscured

Allows them to focus purely on

What life means most to them

An ocean of serene calm

Washing all over their bodies

Cleansing deep to the core

Stimulating senses from lives lived

Hundreds of years before

With each step

And every breath they both take

They appreciate the power

Of a myriad of subtle moments

Engulfing them, bit by bit

Dining on each other's company

For they know no fear

Their hearts are filled

With so much more, complete euphoria

Wandering off into the languorous sunset

Taking new adventures in their stride

Nothing can hurt them as they remain

Side by side, forever entwined

Purfect Players
April 2014

In Ancient Egypt, they were once revered

Their ability to kill vermin was highly praised

Now that they're fully domesticated

At times they can be just plain annoying

Leaving me a plethora of presents galore

Some of them smelling worse than dirty laundry

Don't get me started when they start partying

Singing and screaming outside of my window

Let's say I want a quick cuddle

If I can grab one running at the speed of light

I will get some mutual affection, no doubt

Until the knives come out if I squeeze too tight

Each one of them unique characters

All with multiple personalities disorders

If they were humans, they would be locked up

Furry felines however, get away with murder

You put more than one of them together

You will certainly have a fight on your hands

But when they know that you are not looking

They will clean each other and be the best of friends

When it's feeding time, which is far too often

It might as well be at the flaming zoo

Whether dry or wet, it's all fair game

Godzilla destroys cities more delicately

Than they scoff down all of their food

Yet I am constantly in awe

How much love these creatures inspire

I will always be their most loyal slave

Despite their size, their power knows no bounds

If they look cute then I'm putty in their hands

Cats and dogs own us all and these lands

Forget presidents, kings or queens

Just try to resist and your life will be boring

Room In My Heart For You
October 2014

The raw excitement of your signature kiss

Passionate pulls of tenderness, pure paradise

Silent words breathlessly exchanged

Tasting your sweet nectar

Off ravenous lips and tongue

There's always room in my heart for you

In this often fickle, misinterpreted world

When you're around

Stars never seem to be far or to fade away

The moon refuses to lose its ancient, incandescent glow

Shining iridescent light brightly across your pretty face

A hedonistic ritual begins its inevitable journey

Hibernation from past mistakes and heartbreaks

No longer necessary

Fleeting memories best left forgotten, buried

For new feelings are stirring desires, deep within

Forging a strong bond, as maternity is to the womb

You infect my senses devilishly, coquettishly

With your exquisite, sensual scent

Peeled fruit, zesty

With a subtle hint of lasciviousness

Exuding delectable perfection

From every pore of your skin

All the way down to the magnificent marrow of your bones

For if a sparrow don't know Jack

I sincerely know a holistic view such as this

There's no such thing as excess

When it comes to loving someone

Sink or swim, you dive in

Indulging in mutual, euphorial adrenaline

That is the nature of the game

It is the very essence of why we play

Why we are such exotic, erotic creatures

And ultimately why love is so extraordinary

Spontaneous Instincts
April 2014

I am an ostrich feather

Riding naked in the breeze

Exposed to the raw elements

Yet ultimately free

I am a cow

Chewing the cud

Drifting into the abstract

At one with my thoughts

I am a macaw

Listening to what people say

I mimic and interpret

Putting on my own spin

In different ways

I am a pencil

Sharpening my wits

Making my mark

Proving that I exist

I am love

I can be blind

Inconsiderate at times

Sometimes I am all you have

Yet, sometimes I am all you need

With love comes hope

In each new day

If I am what I say I am

I can be anything to anyone

Truth is no longer a ruin

An inconvenient curse or a burden

I am compassion

And I've completed my mission

Stone Cold Devotion
April 2014

You, I see you arching your eyebrows at me

Our love is but a mere stone's throw away

I marvel at the marble of your exquisite eyes

We are building foundations, a relationship of stone

Let me support you in your hour of need

I'll be waiting for your call, solid, dependable

Never failing to help shape our own destinies

Often simple yet with considerable complexity

We've changed, growing stronger with adaptability

Rocking each other's world in complete harmony

Taking the rough and turning it into smooth

Now we both have the passion of animals

Carving our way together through the world

We found each other through abstract design

A blueprint for a crazy, whirlwind romance

One kiss from you and the walls come crashing down

Quietly reserved yet with a level of sophistication

Every time I look at you, The Renaissance beckons

A statue to match a vision of the Goddesses themselves

You are Venus, older than civilisation itself

Maybe in many years, we will look back

Comparing the material with the physical

Delighting in our decisions based on truths

Architecture starts by placing two bricks together

That's where the spark begins

Where it becomes a flame

Form follows function

And life takes on a more purposeful light

The Sweetest Of All Sounds
May 2015

As myth becomes more potently stronger than knowledge

Where exposure to dreams and goals forge realities

A heart which cannot live without passion perpetually burns

Nothing is more elegantly perfect than perfectly complex

Reflections of ourselves change with the times

In the beginning, we twist to fit our own image

Convinced that material goods and wealth are important

When freedom is more appropriate than possessions

Daring to reveal yourself fully is a daunting task

Yet knowing you always lose when holding back helps

Our ancestors were and still are the greatest encouragers

We can evolve just like they did

Instead of hiding in the shadows

You can create yourself out of a set of noble values

It should not be our purpose to become each other

Be the unique light in the lives of those we care about

The story of love is one of hello and not goodbye

And if life chooses to take what we love so dearly away

Be it through hate, fear or simply death and tragedy

We must be the ones to make that courageous step

To move on and to get closer to other alternatives

Someone else deserving to bridge the gap

Filling our hearts and minds for all eternity

The sweetest of all sounds is one of vulnerability

Taking Euphoria For Granted
January 2013

Instances build tension and then release

Ragged in nature, allocated, jigsaw piece

Adhering to a structure, layered in chaos

Rigid, inhibited until it's simply ridiculous

Facing off to fearsome characters alone

Archetypal of a stereotypical TV show

Sinister undertones, underdog vindication

Riddles, questions manifest without reason

Throwing bouquets right into the firing line

Trust that's contextual, ineffectual, contrived

Balance can represent a worthy challenge if

You're an ignorant bystander in your own life

The monsters that we feed in our psyche

Grow stronger gorging on our own apathy

Burden of proof buried, lying deep within us

To start from scratch as brand new beginners

Brewing a fusion of blood, sweat and tears

Friendship through kismet, kinship, it endures

Playing through each other, a solid symphony

Harnessing the eclectic, an energetic epiphany

Struggling in our bubbles, yearning to be free

Chained, scars remain, flaunted so gloriously

Old fashioned values, extremely rare currency

An ancient fallacy in times of wanton frugality

At the heart of it all, the beating of its core

Pernickety in nature, destined to be flawed

Austerity of the moment, fleeting concerto

An elusive euphoria can be a formidable foe

Appropriate to appreciate how good it can be

Stumbling, head over heels, love's debauchery

Perfect imperfection, with flaws to be seized

For what is love if not at times misconceived

The Tenderness Of Words (AKA Acrostalyptica Part 3)
April 2014

A, you are amazing, I adore you, my adulation knows no bounds

B, you are so beautiful, bountiful, a fragrant bouquet to the senses

C, you are charismatic, so cool, coy, classically, sensuously curvaceous

D, you are determined, dignified, a dancing, dramatic, demure distraction

E, you are elegant, eclectic, so easy going and entrancing

F, you are fabulous, your figure facilitates friendly feelings of freedom

G, you are so gorgeous, generous to a fault, giddy with gentle glee

H, you are humble in your endeavours, heroic, hypnotic, you make me happy

I, you are insightful, imaginative, inspirational and idolized

J, you are a jewel, a jaunty jamboree if ever I did see one

K, you are such a kinky thing, a killer kisser and king of karaoke

L, you are luscious, layered in loveliness, lustfully liberating

M, you are magnificent, molten lava, making my mind melt melodiously

N, you are so natural, nurturing, nectar of the Gods, overwhelmingly nourishing

O, you are opulent, frequently orgasmic, often outsmarting the competition

P, you are perfect, particularly when being playful with your panache

Q, you are quixotic, quick witted, you make me quiver with clever quotes

R, you are romantic, relaxing in the extreme, remarkable how you build rapport

S, you are so succulent, sanguine demeanour shines through, so silky smooth

T, you are thrilling, a typhoon of treacle, flowing strong and true

U, you are undulating, you unclasp your umbrella and we float away together

V, you are soft velvet, vigorously volcanic yet viscerally vivid to the touch

W, you are wicked in wanton ways that writhe all over me, full of woozy warmth

X, you are hard to fathom, even with detailed X-Rays but you still fascinate me

Y, you are full of yearnings, you are most yummy when you are just being you

Z, you are zestful, a zephyr in my ear, the sweetest kiss and then you disappear

A Treasured Night To Remember
April 2014

Just one glass of champagne

Can make us do crazy things

When I'm with you

Life can be so beautiful

I don't want rush this at all

First we'll start out the night

Taking in the magnificent sights

Dancing the night away

Searching Google Maps relentlessly

Especially now the format has changed

Until we find a restaurant we want

That has those little bread sticks

And vol au vonts you like so much

I have no need to complain

You never fail to entertain

After we've worked our way through

A bottle of White and then Rosé too

It's time for us to celebrate

Finishing things off with

Dainty chocolate cheesecakes

Champagne is finally on the menu

The buzz and the thrill

As it tickles our nostrils

Sparkling relentlessly

As vigorously as the aquamarines

Yearning, burning, in your passionate gaze

Then more champers for the ride home

Spending time admiring the stars

And if anyone tries to mug us

We'll introduce the business end

Of a spare bottle to the poor sap's skull

Stepping over his twitching body

Holding hands and laughing

Because we forgot to pay the bill

Life can sometimes be so cruel

But tonight, we're both having a ball!

Wasted Days
April 2014

Well, it's such a useless waste

As the rain pours down your face

Obscuring messages

That disappear down the drain

A fish out of water

In a foreign town, across the border

There's so many words and gestures

That go unanswered

Whispered blindly into the wind

I cannot help but be entranced

As smiles play across your sweet lips

Courage is in such short supply

When your gorgeous gaze hits my eyes

My heart, I know that it can't cope

When you sit so close

My stomach

Spins and somersaults

A daredevil out of control

Yet, I find a will of iron within

To take you gently by the hand

All these tears that you've been crying

The rain washes them all away

In the past, you've been hurt

That was then, they were all idiots

To take a chance

To trust someone

The hardest thing

That can be done

But these wasted days

Can't go on

The past is behind us

Long forgotten

Live for now

Can't you see

Set yourself free

Take a chance on me

Some day, some day, some day

We're Not Chasing Rainbows Anymore
January 2013

Entranced by her measured, wayward glance

A romantic bullet shoots deep into my heart

While I'm vulnerable, exposed, a target

She's a gazelle frolicking in the forest

Bathing in this electric atmosphere

A mysterious creature with an agenda

Falling madly in love with her vibrant nature

Dangerous when ardour is the negotiator

Her arm brushes briefly against mine

Soft as a feather, tethered, entwined

The nape and glorious shape of her neck

Makes me shiver, quivering on the vine

We gather our drinks to aid courage

Smiling a mile wide, while our eyes collide

Hearts fluttering, erratic butterflies

Diving headlong into this tumultuous ride

Babbling like brooks to each other's ocean

Ties that bind, drive our lustful emotions

Speech flows errantly, frothy, no longer raw

We're not chasing rainbows anymore

Fragments of our once empty lives

Now filled with colour, texture and spice

Peppered, wild, on fire, invoking the spirit

Dirty essence of aloneness now banished

Will this relationship serve its purpose?

Take us to far away, exotic places

Seeds, foundation, potential are all there

Ingredients required for a thrilling adventure

And if change were to rear its ugly head

After years passed, marked, full of promises

Seize each other and don't look back

For time is the enemy of a bitter man

If you revere her, the world is your oyster

Remember what brought you here

Let her love refill your endless reservoir

And I guarantee you'll adore each day more

Or your money back

CPSIA information can be obtained at www.ICGtesting.com
Printed in the USA
LVOW07s2340010816

498623LV00001B/216/P

9 781523 676675